Can’t Get Her Ou[illegible]

A Kylie Minogue Trivia Book

By

Etienne di Cosimo

Copyright © 2014 by Dream Song Productions

All Rights Reserved

A Diva Galore Mini-Book

For Mateo…

And especially for Kylie, for bringing so much joy to so many lives. Thanks for everything you do!

Pop Goddess. Diva. International Superstar. Soap Star. Fashion and Style Icon. Gay Icon. Sex Symbol. Humanitarian. Cancer Survivor. Fair Dinkum Aussie Girl.

These superlatives can be used to describe only one person: The incandescent Kylie (no last name required)!

Can't Get Her Out of My Head: A **Kylie Minogue** Trivia Book by Etienne di Cosimo is the ultimate love letter written for **Kylie's** millions of fans from around the world, celebrating the life of one of the most beloved entertainers of all time.

So go ahead, test your knowledge of the adorably loveable **Princess of Pop!**

The Kylie Trivia Challenge

1. The sexy video to Kylie's hit song "Slow" was filmed in what beautiful and cosmopolitan European city?

a) Lisbon, Portugal

b) Barcelona, Spain

c) Rome, Italy

d) Athens, Greece

2. One of Kylie's first hits, "The Locomotion", is a remake of a song by what 1960s singer?

____

3. Kylie performed the duet "Kids" with what former member of boy band Take That?

____

4. Kylie appeared in the movie version of what violent 90s video game?

____

5. There have been four wax work models of Kylie displayed at what world-famous museum?

____

6. Kylie was awarded what prestigious honor by Prince Charles at Buckingham Palace in 2008?

____

7. Kylie appeared in a 2007 episode of what classic sci-fi series?

____

8. What Australian city is Kylie's hometown?

a) Brisbane, Queensland

b) Adelaide, South Australia

c) Melbourne, Victoria

d) Sydney, New South Wales

9. Kylie is featured on the single "Higher" by what male UK artist?

____

10. Kylie recorded a version of what Christmas classic (originally performed by Eartha Kitt and later by Madonna) for her *A Kylie Christmas* album?

____

11. A popular mash-up features "Can't Get You Out of My Head" mixed with what classic 80s New Order song?

____

12. What is the title of the 2007 documentary about Kylie, directed by her good friend William Baker, detailing her return to the Showgirl tour after her successful battle with cancer?

____

13. Kylie's sister Dannii appeared on what rival Aussie soap to *Neighbours*?

____

14. Which Kylie album is named for the Greek Goddess of Love?

____

15. What 90s singing star co-wrote and co-produced the smash single "Can't Get You Out of My Head"?

a) Cathy Dennis

b) Donna Lewis

c) CeCe Peniston

d) Martika

16. Kylie had a long-term relationship with what handsome French actor/model?

____

17. What is the name of Kylie's signature designer perfume?

____

18. Kylie scored one of her first big hits with the duet "Especially for You" with which of her *Neighbours* co-stars?

____

19. Which song is Kylie's biggest hit internationally?

____

20. Which hit title is a French language phrase?

____

21. Of the following singers, who **DID NOT** also star on the soap opera *Neighbours*?

a) Natalie Imbruglia

b) Delta Goodrem

c) Holly Valance

d) Olivia Newton-John

22. Complete the title of Kylie's 2006 children's book, *The Showgirl* ____________________.

23. A balloon in the shape of what animal can be seen flying high in the sky in the video to “All the Lovers”?

a) giraffe

b) elephant

c) tiger

d) koala bear

24. What openly gay singer/songwriter praised his affection for Kylie, calling her the “anti-Madonna”?

____

25. What term does Kylie affectionately use to describe her fans?

____

26. Kylie was a featured artist on the re-recording of what classic Band Aid tune in 1989 to raise money for charity?

____

27. Kylie had a cameo appearance as herself in a 1994 episode of what Dawn French Britcom?

____

28. Kylie had a loving, long-term relationship with what sexy Catalan male model?

a) Marc Clotet

b) Jon Kortajarena

c) Antonio Navas

d) Andrés Velencoso Segura

29. Kylie appeared as what character on the iconic soap opera *Neighbours*?

____

30. What brand of European luxury sports car is Kylie driving in the "Can't Get You Out of My Head" video?

a) De Tomaso Mangusta

b) Alfa Romeo Spider Quadrifoglio

c) Maserati Quattroporte

d) Lamborghini Aventador

31. Kylie made an appearance as the Green Fairy in what Baz Luhrman directed musical film?

____

32. What handsome French actor/model appeared as Kylie's passionate lover in the video for her hit song "Into the Blue"?

____

33. Following her cancer treatment, Kylie recorded a digital-medium-only release of what classic song made famous by Judy Garland?

____

34. Kylie recorded the duet "Limpido" with what Italian singing star?

____

35. Kylie was one of the featured artists on the charity recording of what classic REM song to raise money for victims of the 2010 earthquake in Haiti?

____

36. Of the following, who **HAS NOT** been a judge on *The Voice UK* talent show?

a) will.i.am

b) Dame Shirley Bassey

c) Sir Tom Jones

d) Ricky Wilson from the Kaiser Chiefs

37. To commemorate her 25th year in the music industry, Kylie recorded a collection of orchestral versions of many of her top hits in an album named after what Beatles' classic?

____

38. Kylie won what Australian acting award in 1987 as Most Popular Actress for her role on the soap opera *Neighbours*?

____

39. Kylie was featured in television advertisements for what health club chain?

____

40. What ABBA song did Kylie perform at the closing ceremonies to the 2000 Summer Olympic Games in Sydney, Australia?

a) “The Winner Takes It All”

b) “Waterloo”

c) “Dancing Queen”

d) “Take a Chance on Me”

41. Kylie recorded a remake of what classic 80s Kool & The Gang tune for her first Greatest Hits collection released in 1992?

____

42. Kylie co-starred with Stephen Baldwin and American comedian Pauly Shore in what 1996 film?

____

43. Kylie recorded the song “Where the Wild Roses Grow” with what acclaimed Australian band?

a) Rose Tattoo

b) Midnight Oil

c) Mental As Anything

d) Nick Cave & The Bad Seeds

44. Kylie had a high-profile romance with Michael Hutchence, the late lead singer of what successful Aussie Rock band?

____

45. Of the following, who **HAS NOT** also been a judge on *The Voice Australia* talent show:

a) Helen Reddy

b) Ricky Martin

c) Joel Madden

d) Keith Urban

46. The hooded white jumpsuit that Kylie famously wore in the unforgettable "Can't Get You Out of My Head" video was on display at the "Kylie: Exhibition" in what prestigious London museum?

____

47. Kylie appeared in the production of what William Shakespeare play during a run on the Caribbean island of Barbados?

a) *Romeo and Juliet*

b) *Othello*

c) *The Tempest*

d) *Macbeth*

48. Kylie was born under what Zodiac star sign? (Hint: Her birthday is May 28).

____

49. The single “I Believe in You” was co-written by what lead singer of the American band The Scissor Sisters?

____

50. On what two Australian soap operas did Kylie and her sister Dannii both star?

____

51. Kylie began her career by performing songs written and produced by what famous musical production team?

____

52. Of the following, which band **WAS NOT** produced by the same musical production team from the above question?

a) Bananarama

b) Rick Astley

c) Dead or Alive

d) New Kids on the Block

53. What High Energy NRG singer recorded her own version of the early-Kylie song “Turn It Into Love”?

____

54. Of the following artists, with whom has Kylie **NOT** collaborated/recorded?

a) Keith Washington

b) Coldplay

c) Lady Gaga

d) Towa Tei

55. A bronze cast of Kylie’s hands is on exhibition in the “Square of Fame” at what legendary London concert venue?

____

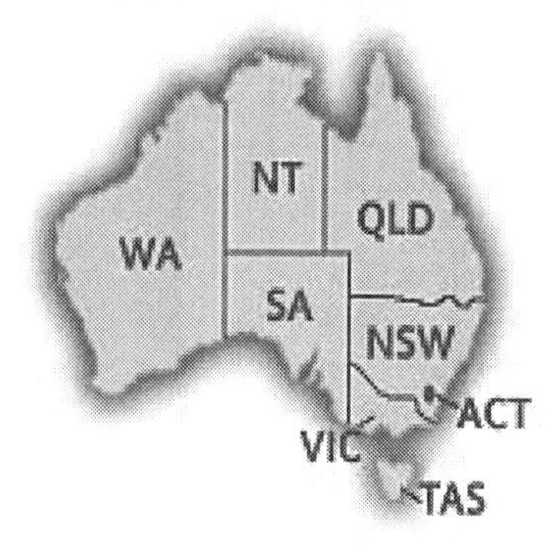

56. What was the title of Kylie's debut Australian movie, released in 1989?

____

57. What is Kylie's middle name?

____

58. “Spinning Around” was co-written by what American pop star, singer of the hits “Straight Up” and “Rush, Rush”?

____

59. Finish the title of the following songs:

a) “Better the ______________ You Know”

b) “On a ______________ Like This”

c) “Your ______________ Needs You”

d) “Tears on My ______________”

e) “It’s No ______________”

f) “Come into My ______________”

g) “2 ______________”

h) “Red Blooded ______________”

60. Which album is her top seller, with over six millions copies sold worldwide?

a) *Fever*

b) *X*

c) *Light Years*

d) *Aphrodite*

61. What ABBA song did Kylie record with her sister Dannii?

____

62. Kylie's 1998 album *Impossible Princess* was re-titled *Kylie Minogue* following the death of what internationally beloved public figure?

____

63. What was the name of the record label that signed Kylie to her very first recording contract in 1987?

a) Roo Records

b) Rhino Record

c) Mushroom Records

d) RCA

64. What is the title of William Baker's photographic biography about his good friend Kylie, published in 2002?

____

65. On what fictional street did Kylie's character live on the popular soap *Neighbours*?

____

66. Which song won the Grammy Award for Best Dance Recording in 2004?

____

67. A parody of Kylie appeared on what 80s-era British comedy series, featuring grotesque puppets fashioned in the images of celebrities?

____

68. What European capital has Kylie called home for over twenty years?

a) London

b) Paris

c) Zurich, Switzerland

d) Dublin, Ireland

69. Kylie and her sister Dannii have both made several appearances at what heralded gay and lesbian event held annually in Sydney?

____

70. Kylie read the lyrics to which one of her songs as a poem during the "Poetry Olympics" held at London's Royal Albert Hall in 1996?

____

List Kylie's Albums in Chronological Order:

A) *Aphrodite*	1. ________
B) *Fever*	2. ________
C) *Rhythm of Love*	3. ________
D) *Kylie*	4. ________
E) *Impossible Princess*	5. ________
F) *Kiss Me Once*	6. ________
G) *Body Language*	7. ________
H) *Enjoy Yourself*	8. ________
I) *Light Years*	9. ________
J) *Let's Get to It!*	10. _______
K) *X*	11. _______
L) *Kylie Minogue*	12. _______

Lyrical Quiz:

Identify the Kylie song that features each of the following lyric lines:

71. "I need your love, like night needs morning."

____

72. "If love were liquid, it would drown me."

____

73. "I'll forgive and forget, if you say you'll never go."

____

74. “Count backwards: 5, 4, 3, 2, 1…before you get too heated and too turned on.”

____

75. “The sand is running quick, right through our hands…”

____

76. “My heart is close to breaking, and I can’t go on faking.”

____

77. “You’re dancing with the chairman of the board.”

____

78. "…And everything went from wrong to right…"

____

79. "Clearin' this house out of joy that I borrowed."

____

80. "I'm not ashamed of all my mistakes, 'cause through the cold I still keep the fire burning."

____

81. "You kiss me, I'm falling…It's your name I'm calling."

____

82. “I wanna tell you I was feeling that way too, and if dreams were wings, you know, I would have flown to you.”

____

83. “Desperately seeking someone willing to travel; You’re lost in conversation and useless at Scrabble.”

____

84. “The joker’s always smiling, in every hand that’s dealt.”

____

85. “We all get hurt by love, and we all have our cross to bear.”

Name the Video

Identify the Kylie video from the following descriptions:

86. Kylie and a number of clones create a scene as they pull a "Groundhog Day" and walk in circles on a busy Parisian street.

____

87. Kylie emulates the ultimate Vargas pinup girl, as she struts her stuff in a club wearing the hottest gold lamé hot pants of all time.

____

88. Kylie appears as a murdered woman from the painting *Ophelia* by renowned artist John Everett Millais.

---

89. Kylie writhes sensuously by an Olympic-sized swimming pool overlooking a European city with a large group of super-sexy, scantily-clad sun worshippers.

---

90. Kylie is adored by scores of hedonistic revelers who strip down to their skivvies and commence making out passionately, forming a pyramid of love with Kylie on top along a Los Angeles Street.

---

91. Kylie the barmaid lends her loser boyfriend money, before taking it back and running off for a head-clearing walkabout in the stunning Aussie bush, strolling along spectacular beaches to rediscover her inner soul.

____

92. Kylie gets impatient and over-heated while caught in an LA traffic jam, jumping out of her car, dancing on a big rig while being escorted by two Dobermans, before changing her clothes in a stranger's vehicle and Hip-Hop dancing in a club.

____

93. Mademoiselle Kylie waits for her errant lover in the rain in a village in France, but quickly starts imagining herself in a 1940s era Gene Kelley musical.

____

94. Kylie and assorted dancers don funky, 70s garb and do the Bus Stop while reminiscing about the good ol' days.

____

95. Kylie transforms into a Goth goddess dressed all in black, vamping it up and singing seductively from atop a piano, *Fabulous Baker Boys* style.

____

True or False

Indicate if the following statements regarding Kylie are **True** or **False**:

96. Kylie was the first Australian female artist to debut at Number One on the UK pop charts with her single "Spinning Around".

____

97. Kylie made an appearance on the cult Australian comedy series *Kath and Kim.*

____

98. Kylie has sold approximately 20 million records internationally.

____

99. Kylie temporarily entered into politics, running unsuccessfully as a mayoral candidate in Melbourne, Australia in 2008.

---

100. UK tabloid *The Sun* ranked Kylie Number One on their list of the greatest gay icons of all time.

101: Kylie’s mentee on *The Voice UK,* Jamie Johnson, won the 2014 competition.

---

102. Kylie is known for her contralto singing voice.

___

103. Kylie has often stated her admiration of pop superstar Madonna, citing her as a major influence over her career.

___

104. One of Kylie's first romances was with her *Neighbours* co-star, Jason Donovan.

___

105. Kylie had to postpone her Aphrodite World Tour after she was diagnosed with breast cancer.

____

106. Kylie was appointed Chevalier of the French Ordre des Arts et des Lettres, one of France's highest cultural honors.

____

107. Kylie made the valiant decision to continue with her Aphrodite World Tour in Japan following the devastating March 2011 earthquake and tsunami.

---

108. Kylie is set to appear in a sequel to the overblown disaster flick *2012*, scheduled for release in 2016.

---

109. Kylie's album *Impossible Princess* was later renamed *Kylie Minogue* following the unexpected death of Diana, Princess of Wales in 1997.

---

110. Kylie was signed to her first record label after performing a duet of the Sonny & Cher standard “I Got You Babe” with a co-star for a charity benefit in 1987.

____

The Answers…

Kylie Trivia Challenge Answers:

1. B, Barcelona, Spain
2. Little Eva
3. Robbie Williams
4. *Street Fighter*
5. Madame Tussaud's
6. OBE, Order of the British Empire
7. *Dr. Who*
8. C. Melbourne
9. Taio Cruz
10. *"Santa, Baby"*

11. *"Blue Monday"*

12. "White Diamond"

13. *Home & Away*

14. *Aphrodite*

15. A, Cathy Dennis

16. Olivier Martinez

17. Darling

18. Jason Donovan

19. *"Can't Get You Out of My Head"*, with over five million copies sold.

20. *"Je Ne Sais Pas Pourquoi"*

21. D, Olivia Newton John

22. Princess

23. B, elephant

24. Rufus Wainwright

25. Lovers

26. *"Do They Know It's Christmas?"*

27. *The Vicar of Dibley*

28. D, Andrés Velencoso Segura

29. Charlene Mitchell Robinson

30. A, De Tomaso Mangusta

31. *Moulin Rouge*

32. Clément Sibony

33. *"Over the Rainbow"*

34. Laura Pausini

35. *"Everybody Hurts"*

36. B, Dame Shirley Bassey

37. *Abbey Road Sessions*

38. The Logie

39. Bally's Total Fitness

40. C, *"Dancing Queen"*

41. *"Celebration"*

42. *Biodome*

43. D, Nick Cave & The Bad Seeds

44. INXS

45. A, Helen Reddy

46. The Victoria and Albert Museum

47. C, *"The Tempest"*

48. Gemini

49. Jake Shears

50. *The Sullivans* and *Skyways*

51. SAW, Stock, Aitken & Waterman

52. D, The New Kids on the Block

53. Hazell Dean

54. C, Lady GaGa

55. Wembley Arena

56. *The Delinquents*

57. Ann

58. Paula Abdul

59. a) Devil

    b) Night

    c) Disco

    d) Pillow

    e) Secret

    f) World

    g) Hearts

    h) Woman

60. A, *Fever*

61. *"The Winner Takes It All"*

62. Princess Diana

63. C, Mushroom Records

64. *Kylie: La La La*

65. Ramsay Street

66. *"Come into My World"*

67. *Spitting Image*

68. A, London

69. Sydney Mardi Gras

70. *"I Should Be So Lucky"*

List Kylie's Albums in Chronological Order of Release:

1. D, *Kylie*
2. H, *Enjoy Yourself*
3. C, *Rhythm of Love*
4. J, *Let's Get to It*
5. L, *Kylie Minogue*
6. E, *Impossible Princess*
7. I, *Light Years*
8. B, *Fever*
9. G, *Body Language*
10. K, *X*
11. A, *Aphrodite*
12. F, *Kiss Me*

Kylie Lyrical Quiz:

71. *"Come into My World"*
72. *"Chocolate"*
73. *"Better the Devil You Know"*
74. *"Red-Blooded Woman"*
75. *"Timebomb"*
76. *"I Should Be So Lucky"*
77. *"Kids"*
78. *"Love at First Sight"*
79. *"Spinning Around"*
80. *"Into the Blue"*
81. *"On a Night Like This"*

82. *"Especially for You"*

83. *"Your Disco Needs You"*

84. *"I Believe in You"*

85. *"Confide in Me"*

Name the Video:

86. *"Come into My World"*
87. *"Spinning Around"*
88. *"Where the Wild Roses Grow"*
89. *"Slow"*
90. *"All the Lovers"*
91. *"It's No Secret"*
92. *"Red-Blooded Woman"*
93. *"Je Ne Sais Pas Pourquoi"*
94. *"Step Back in Time"*
95. *"2 Hearts"*

True or False:

96. True

97. True

98. False. Kylie has sold over 70 million records during the course of her career.

99. False

100. True

101. False. will.i.am's selection Jermain Jackman won.

102. False. Her voice registers in the soft soprano range.

103. True

104. True

105. False. It was during her "Showgirl" tour.

106. True

107. True

108. False, although Kylie has signed on to appear in *San Andreas,* an earthquake disaster movie co-starring Dwayne "The Rock" Johnson.

109. True

110. True

About the Author

Etienne di Cosimo is a pop culture expert and the author of *Can't Get You Out of My Head: A Kylie Minogue Trivia Book* and *The Rise of CR7: A Cristiano Ronaldo Trivia Book.* He divides his time between the South of France and New York City.